DOG ON A LOG™
Let's GO! Books
Step 5

This is a work of fiction. Names, characters, places, and incidents are either products of the author's imagination or are used fictitiously. Any resemblance to actual persons, living or dead, businesses, companies, events, or locales is entirely coincidental.

DOG ON A LOG Books
Tucson, Arizona

FIVE
LET'S GO!
BOOKS
5

A companion to
FIVE CHAPTER BOOKS 5

DOG ON A LOG Let's GO! Books
Step 5

By Pamela Brookes

Download DOG ON A LOG printable gameboards, games, flashcards, and other activities at:
www.dogonalogbooks.com/printables.

Parents and Teachers:
Receive email notifications of new books and printables. Sign up at:
www.dogonalogbooks.com/subscribe

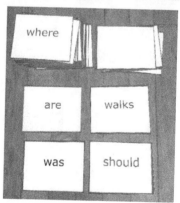

Table of Contents

DOG ON A LOG
Parent and Teacher Guides

General Information on Dyslexia and Struggling Readers

The Author's Routine for Teaching Reading

Book 1. *Teaching a Struggling Reader: One Mom's Experience with Dyslexia*

Book 2. *How to Use Decodable Books to Teach Reading*

Available for free from many online booksellers or read at:
www.dogonalogbooks.com/free

BAKE A CAKE

CAKE RECIPE
INCLUDED

"Jan, do you want to help me bake a cake?" Mom asks. "The stuff for the cake is on the shelf."

"We must have eggs for the cake. Go get eggs from Pine Cone the hen," Mom says.

An egg drops at the gate. It broke. The hens want it for lunch.

"We will make the cake from nuts. We must crush the nuts," says Mom.

NUT
CRUSH
THING

Mom puts the cake in to bake. When the bell rings it will be time to check the cake.

Mom gets red pads to lift the pan from the rack.

She sets the pan on a plate.

Kate Tate is in bed. She fell and broke her hip.

Jan, Mom, and Kate Tate have cake. Kate Tate smiles. Jan is glad that she and Mom made Kate Tate a cake.

Almond Orange Cake with Chocolate Chips Recipe

NUT ALLERGIES:
You can substitute 6 oz ground shelled raw unsalted pumpkin seeds and 1/2 cup ground flax seeds for the almond flour.

Ingredients:
14 ounces Clementines or Oranges
6 large Eggs (2 ounces each)
1/3 cup Honey
2 cups Almond Flour
1 ½ tsp Baking Powder
1/2 tsp Salt
1 1/3 cups Chocolate Chips (optional)

Directions:

Wash then boil the clementines or oranges until they are soft when pierced by a fork. This can take anywhere from 30 to 90 minutes depending on the size of the fruit. Allow the oranges to cool. Blending hot oranges with eggs could cause the eggs to change consistency.

Preheat oven to 300 degrees. Cut a piece of parchment paper about 7 1/2" x 8 ¾." Lightly oil the inside of a cast iron or glass bread pan. Place parchment paper so it covers the long sides and bottom of the bread pan.

Place the boiled oranges, eggs and honey in a blender and blend until smooth. Mix the Almond Flour, Baking Powder, and Salt in a batter bowl. Add the mixture from the blender and stir until smooth. Add in the chocolate chips and stir until the chips are evenly distributed.

Scoop the batter into the prepared bread pan being careful not to get the batter between the parchment and the pan. Carefully jiggle the pan so the batter completely fills the corners and there are no air pockets and the top of the batter is level and smooth. You may want to place a few chocolate chips on top in a decorative fashion.

Bake for 30 minutes then lightly cover the pan with a piece of foil, parchment, or silicone. If you placed chocolate chips on top of the batter, be careful to not smash the chips. If you use foil you can make a tent that raises a bit above the pan.

Bake for another 45-60 minutes or so until a baking thermometer inserted into the middle of the loaf reads about 205 to 210. Because this is a moist cake I like to get it closer to 210 degrees. Total baking time will be about to 1 hour 15 minutes to 1 ½ hours. This is a dense cake so baking can take a while. Remove and allow to cool. Remove loaf from pan, slice, and serve.

FOR A SWEETER CAKE use just 1 ½ cups almond flour or 4 oz ground pumpkin seeds and 1/3 cup ground flax. Reduce baking time to an hour or so.

Sight Words used in "Bake A Cake"

a, be, do, egg, eggs, for, from, go, have, her, is, me, puts, says, she, the, to, want, we, you

Approximately 135 words

THE CRANE
AT THE CAVE

Quin and Dave are in the back lot of their home.

Their dog, Bade, takes them to the gate and up a hill.

Bade jumps to a rock. He digs a hole. He sees a cave.

"Bade dug a big cave," Dave tells Mom and Dad.

"We should ride bikes to see it," Mom says.

There is a crate and a bed in the cave.

"We must get a crane," Dad says.

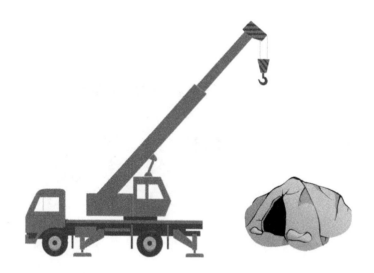

The crane boss goes into the cave. He gets the crane rope on the crate.

"OK. You can winch the crate up," the crane boss yells.

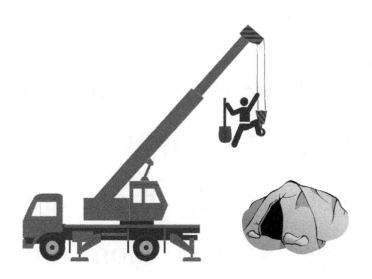

"The cave is on your land. That makes this your crate," the crane boss says to Mom and Dad.

The crane boss sets the bed on the back of the crane. The crane lifts the crate. They drive the crane to their home.

There are quilts and a plush dog and cat in the crate. Quin and Dave will take naps with them in the bed.

Sight Words used in "The Crane at the Cave"

a, are, goes, he, into, is, of, OK, says, see, sees, should, the, their, there, they, to, we, you, your

Approximately 165 words

RIDE A BIKE

Jan's home is on top of a hill. She likes to see a finch, bob cats, snakes, bats, and sand frogs.

Jan gets on her bike and rides up the hill. It is in back of her home.

Jan's dad likes to ride his bike. Jan's dog, Tup, likes to run with the bikes.

Jan thinks her bike
is a tame elk. Tup runs
at her side.

"When it is just kids, dogs can say lots of stuff," Tup says.

"It is the same with elk," the elk says.

"I see a snake," Tup says.

"What luck," Jan says.

"I want to be safe. Go home!" the snake says.

Al the elk and Tup the dog run fast to get home.

Al the elk goes.
Mom and Dad just see
a bike.

Jan, Mom, and Dad have a snack.

Tup chomps a fig.

Jan sits in Dad's lap.

She likes her home.

Sight Words used in "RIDE A BIKE"

a, be, go, goes, have, her, his, I, is, of, say, says, see, she, the, to, want, what

Approximately 150 words

CRANE OR CRANE?

"Mom, can I get a crane?" I ask.

"What do you want a crane for?" she says.

"I could take a bath with it. And I could dig with it. And I could hiss with it," I say.

"A crane would get rid of the bugs," I say.

"The bad smell would chase the bugs from home. Still, a crane is not a fine plan," Mom says.

"What would you do with a crane?" Mom says.

"I would hug it and pet it," I say.

"You would hug it? Or would you sit on it?" Mom says.

"I would not sit on a crane," I say.

"Where would you put a crane?" she asks.

"It would be in the hen pen," I say.

"The hens would sit on the crane," Mom says.

"Not if the crane flaps its wings," I say.

Mom smiles. "You want a crane with wings. If you want a pet I will get you a rat," she says.

Sight Words used in "Crane or Crane?"

a, could, do, for, from, I, is, of, or, put, say, says, she, the, want, what, where, would, you

Approximately 160 words

THE SWING GATE

Gabe likes the swing gate. He can not tell what the gate will be.

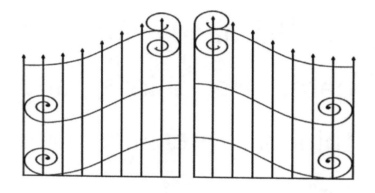

His hands grab the gate. He thinks and thinks. Where will he go?

He is on a small ship. He is in a cove.

The ship hits the sand with a thud. He goes to the top of the sand hill.

He runs to a maze.
A bug says, "When you
see the kite you get to
munch cake."

Gabe sees a chick. The chick says, "You must go left if you want to see the kite."

Gabe walks and walks in the maze. There are bugs on the brick wall.

A mink runs up to Gabe. "The kite is at the end of the sand," the mink says. "I will take you there."

Gabe sees the kite.
"Here is your cake,"
the mink says.

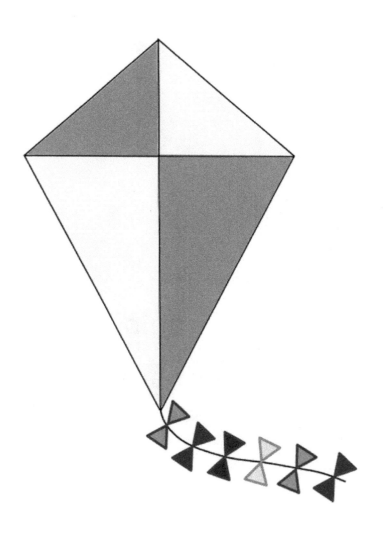

Gabe has his cake then goes back to the ship. The ship takes him to the gate. He is home.

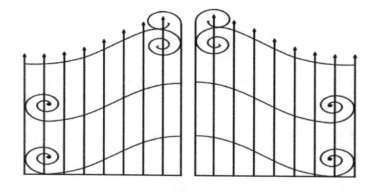

Sight Words used in "The Swing Gate"

a, are, be, go, goes, has, he, here, his, is, I, is, of, says, see, sees, the, there, to, walks, want, what, where, you, your

Approximately 160 words

DOG ON A LOG Books
Phonics Progression

DOG ON A LOG Pup Books
Book 1
Phonological/Phonemic Awareness:
- Words
- Rhyming
- Syllables, identification, blending, segmenting
- Identifying individual letter sounds

Books 2-3
Phonemic Awareness/Phonics
- Consonants, primary sounds
- Short vowels
- Blending
- Introduction to sight words

DOG ON A LOG Let's GO! and Chapter Books

Step 1
- Consonants, primary sounds
- Short vowels
- Digraphs: ch, sh, th, wh, ck
- 2 and 3 sound words
- Possessive 's

Step 2
- Bonus letters (f, l, s, z after short vowel)
- "all"
- −s suffix

Step 3
- Letter Buddies: ang, ing, ong, ung, ank, ink, onk, unk

Step 4
- Consonant blends to make 4 sound words
- 3 and 4 sound words ending in −lk, -sk

Step 5
- Digraph blend −nch to make 3 and 4 sound words
- Silent e, including "-ke"

Step 6
- Exception words containing: ild, old, olt, ind, ost

Step 7
- 5 sounds in a closed syllable word plus suffix -s (crunch, slumps)
- 3 letter blends and up to 6 sounds in a closed syllable word (script, spring)

Step 8

- Two-syllable words with 2 closed syllables, not blends (sunset, chicken, unlock)

Step 9

- Two-syllable words with all previously introduced sounds including blends, exception words, and silent "e" (blacksmith, kindness, inside)
- Vowel digraphs: ai, ay, ea, ee, ie, oa, oe (rain, play, beach, tree, pie, boat, toe)

WATCH FOR MORE STEPS COMING SOON

Let's GO! Books have less text

Chapter Books are longer

DOG ON A LOG Books
Sight Word Progression

DOG ON A LOG Pup Books

a, does, go, has, her is, of, says, the, to

DOG ON A LOG Let's GO! and Chapter Books

Step 1
a, and, are, be, does, go, goes, has, he, her, his, into, is, like, my, of, OK, says, see, she, the, they, to, want, you

Step 2
could, do, eggs, for, from, have, here, I, likes, me, nest, onto, or, puts, said, say, sees, should, wants, was, we, what, would, your

Step 3
as, Mr., Mrs., no, put, their, there, where

Step 4
push, saw

Step 5
come, comes, egg, pull, pulls, talk, walk, walks

Step 6
Ms., so, some, talks

Step 7
Hmmm, our, out, Pop E., TV

Step 8
Dr., friend, full, hi, island, people, please

More DOG ON A LOG Books

Most books available in Paperback, Hardback, and e-book formats

DOG ON A LOG Parent and Teacher Guides

Book 1 (Also in FREE e-book and PDF Bookfold)
- Teaching a Struggling Reader: One Mom's Experience with Dyslexia

Book 2 (FREE e-book and PDF Bookfold only)
- How to Use Decodable Books to Teach Reading

DOG ON A LOG Pup Books
Book 1
- Before the Squiggle Code (A Roadmap to Reading)

Books 2-3
- The Squiggle Code (Letters Make Words)
- Kids' Squiggles (Letters Make Words)

DOG ON A LOG Let's GO! and Chapter Books

Step 1
- The Dog on the Log
- The Pig Hat
- Chad the Cat
- Zip the Bug
- The Fish and the Pig

Step 2
- Mud on the Path
- The Red Hen
- The Hat and Bug Shop
- Babs the 'Bot
- The Cub

Step 3
- Mr. Bing has Hen Dots
- The Junk Lot Cat
- Bonk Punk Hot Rod
- The Ship with Wings
- The Sub in the Fish Tank

Step 4
- The Push Truck
- The Sand Hill
- Lil Tilt and Mr. Ling
- Musk Ox in the Tub
- The Trip to the Pond

Step 5
- Bake a Cake
- The Crane at the Cave
- Ride a Bike
- Crane or Crane?
- The Swing Gate

Step 6
- The Colt
- The Gold Bolt
- Hide in the Blinds
- The Stone Child
- Tolt the Kind Cat

Step 7
- Quest for A Grump Grunt
- The Blimp
- The Spring in the Lane
- Stamp for a Note
- Stripes and Splats

Step 8
- Anvil and Magnet
- The Mascot
- Kevin's Rabbit Hole
- The Humbug Vet and Medic Shop
- Chickens in the Attic

Step 9
- Trip to Cactus Gulch 1: The Step-Up Team
- Trip to Cactus Gulch 2: Into the Mineshaft
- Play the Bagpipes
- The Hidden Tale 1: The Lost Snapshot

All chapter books can be purchased individually or with all the same-step books in one volume.

Steps 1-5 can be bought as Let's GO! Books which are less text companions to the chapter books.

All titles can be bought as chapter books.

WATCH FOR MORE BOOKS COMING SOON

How You Can Help

Parents often worry that their child (or even adult learner) is not going to learn to read. Hearing other people's successes (especially when they struggled) can give worried parents or teachers hope. I would encourage others to share their experiences with products you've used by posting reviews at your favorite bookseller(s) stating how your child benefitted from those books or materials (whether it was DOG ON A LOG Books or another book or product.) This will help other parents and teachers know which products they should consider using. More than that, hearing your successes could truly help another family feel hopeful. It's amazing that something as seemingly small as a review can ease someone's concerns.

DOG ON A LOG Quick Assessment

Have your child read the following words. If they can't read every word in a Step, that is probably where in the series they should start. Get a printable assessment sheet at: www.dogonalogbooks.com/how-to-use/ assessment-tool/

Step 1
fin, mash, sock, sub, cat, that, Dan's

Step 2
less, bats, tell, mall, chips, whiff, falls

Step 3
bangs, dank, honk, pings, chunk, sink, gong, rungs

Step 4
silk, fluff, smash, krill, drop, slim, whisk

Step 5
hunch, crate, rake, tote, inch, mote, lime

Step 6
child, molts, fold, hind, jolt, post, colds

Step 7
strive, scrape, splint, twists, crunch, prints, blend

Step 8
finish, denim, within, bathtub, sunset, medic, habit

Step 9
hundred, goldfinch, free, wheat, inhale, play, Joe

CPSIA information can be obtained
at www.ICGtesting.com
Printed in the USA
BVHW031826110521
607062BV00011B/82